CrowdFunding in a Nutshell

Joy Alatta

Copyrights

Published by **WriteOn Publishers**.

Copyright 2014

For information, contact:
'copyright@ijobers.com'

ISBN-13: 978-1499270020

ISBN-10: 149927002X

Table of Contents

Preface

Small businesses are known to be the highest employer of labor in many economies of the world. The impact of small business support to economic growth is by no means a small one. Yet small businesses are still left out in the cold and are lacking greatly in areas of startup funds and later stage financing. In some countries, small business jobs account for about 50% to 80% of all jobs. That is an indication that lack of growth in small businesses can hamper economic growth. The need to ensure that small businesses have access to finance is an urgent issue that needs to be addressed as a matter of priority.

Every entrepreneur needs the right operating environment like access to finance and business advisors to enable them continue to foster economic growth. It is worthy to note that small businesses employ local residents and thus create unique sense of belonging to individuals. The effect is that quality of life of individuals are enhanced through employment and the business has a better chance of surviving challenges because employees feel committed to make it work.

Recent economic woes plaguing the world have led to increase in the number of people wanting to start their own business. This caused an increase in frustrations and challenges experienced by small businesses who want to secure business funding.

It is still surprising to know that despite all discussions and agenda of various governments around the world, there has been a very little impact on helping small businesses secure business funding. It seems that banks are still unyielding and more determined to reject small business application for loans and overdraft.

Why you need to know about crowdfunding

While entrepreneurs and small businesses are struggling to stay afloat, and banks are being blamed for the difficulties of small businesses to secure business lending, it is important to note that banks are not left out of the recession waves blowing across the globe. What is even more challenging is the lack of information and knowledge about alternative source of business finance. Many small businesses are still hanging on to the traditional belief that only banks can facilitate business finance. A report by Experian (Credit Agency) confirmed that many small business owners are yet to know that they can secure business finance through other sources.

In the past, it is a very difficult task to get information on any topic. In most cases it would require a visit to the library. All that has changed dramatically due to the power of the internet. Dissemination of information has become very easily available through various means. The power of the internet to harness and pull resources and information from likeminded people has facilitated the generation of creative and alternative means of raising finance for just any venture.

Crowdfunding is one of such alternative means of raising finance from the crowd. The internet has made geographical locations irrelevant because it created a global paying ground where people connect virtually to collaborate and interact and invest. Crowdfunding is the buzz word that has been giving a meaning when a group of likeminded people drawn together by the power of the internet can make individual decision to support a project. There are no limits to the kind of project that can be supported through crowdfunding. It could be business, philanthropic, not for profit, individual dreams or passion.

The exciting part of crowdfunding is that when an entrepreneur or a small business harnesses the benefits of crowdfunding, the business is no more at the mercy of banks and other main stream lending organizations. Amazing results are been achieved by ordinary people who tapped into the benefit of the internet to secure funds from diverse group of people in various geographic locations.

I am a big proponent of crowdfunding because of the ability of entrepreneurs and small businesses to have access to capital which they need to turn their ideas into a reality. It means that just anyone, anywhere can have the same opportunity to raise funds and likewise anyone anywhere can make a personal decision to support worthy projects.

There are without doubt some challenges in crowdfunding but there are indications that crowdfunding platforms and industry regulators are developing approaches to mitigate those challenges. In the recent developments it has been noted that "sophisticated" and traditional investors have become involved in the crowdfunding sector.

Why I wrote the book

There is a very wide gap between what crowdfunding is doing and what people know about crowdfunding. Even among those that know about crowdfunding, the level of knowledge of crowdfunding and its industry is still at an elementary level. This could also be the cause of some scattered incidents of were crowdfunding went bad. Crowdfunding industry is young and it is still growing. The growth will continue even as the controversy about it continues to increase.

Most of the books that are already in the market about crowdfunding are based on practices on specific crowdfunding portals. I realized that there is a need to have a book that will expound the topic of crowdfunding with best practices concept. Whatever crowdfunding portal you decide to use, this book will provide a good foundation to enable you demand the best from the portal.

What is covered in the book?

Chapter 1
What is Crowdfunding?

Crowdfunding industry only started to shoot into the lime light in 2009. By the end of 2013, it is estimated to have become a multi-billion dollar industry. The industry has an eco-system of players from different dimensions including innovators, entrepreneurs, inventors, civil societies, financial institution, technology providers, legal professionals and other traditional financial institutions.

The new concept of raising money from the crowd will solve several pressing problems facing both profit and not for profit organizations. With crowdfunding, it is now possible for people to create their own jobs. With your ingenuity, you can grow a micro business into a mega business employing several hundreds of people.

The part I find most interesting is that everyday people who are serving their communities daily can have the opportunity to do more for humanity. These are people that add value to the life of the common man. Inventions that research and development experts gave a vote of no confidence can now see the light of day through the wisdom of the crowd.

This disruptive buzz called crowdfunding has already started changing the equation of who decides what gets funded and what does not get funded. The crowd can now decide what is good for the masses. It is no more industry experts sitting in their comfortable offices to make decisions that boost their profitability. Power to make investment decisions has moved to the people – the crowd.

Crowdfunding is the pulling together of contributions from a diverse group of people with the intention to achieve a stated objective. The contribution could be free, interest bearing, for investment or gratuitous reward. There is no limit to the breadth, span and depth of what crowdfunding could be used to achieve. However, the center focus of the contribution must be legally accepted objective in a given geographical location. The morality of the objective is subject to personal interpretation and may determine who become a contributor and the extent of the acceptability of the objective to the general public.

Though crowdfunding has come to be mostly identified with entrepreneurs and business startups that need funding to achieve their dreams and passions. It does not imply in any way that crowdfunding can only be used for business related projects or objectives.

Crowdfunding is similar to crowdsourcing in a way. Crowdsourcing refers to solving a given problem or achieving a given objective by breaking the task into small bits to a large set of people. The collective effort of large group of people are required for support, the objective of the projects must be clearly articulated and explained to the crowd in a way to elicit the support of crowd.

Fundraising is another related concept to crowdfunding. In fundraising, a not for profit charity body or organization articulates problems that they want to resolve and generate a campaign to elicit support of the general public who identified with their objective. A major difference is that fundraising is strictly for charity while crowdfunding can be used both profit and non- profit purpose. Crowdfunding stands out clearly from fundraising in another instance due to the modes of operation. Fundraising can be done offline and online, but crowdfunding as it is done today is still identified only as an online activity where the project owner uses the power of the internet and social communities to harness financial resources from the crowd.

In crowdfunding, there are intermediaries that moderate the collection of funds and act as a regulatory enforcer of acceptable actions and activities in a crowdfunding project. In fundraising, it is the charity organization that determines how to manage their fundraising activities within the framework of the body regulating charities in a given locality.

Importance of crowdfunding

Finance is the ultimate decider of what gets done and does not get done. There are so many people, groups of people, organizations and even communities who have very noble, economic and humanitarian ideas to implement and use it to make world a better place. The single major reason why so many of these ideas could not be put into practice is because of lack of financial support.

Business owners are not left of the negative impact of lack of financial support. This is because banks and other financial related institutions are the major source of securing any form of finance. Crowdfunding is lending economic hand and supporting individuals and organizations to generate and secure much needed finance. It is a well known fact that finance is the life blood of any business, society and even governments.

Crowdfunding has continued to create new jobs and improve quality of life of many local communities. Individuals who have invested in crowdfunding projects are happy to keep on investing when they see the impact of their contribution in their local communities. Crowdfunding is a very good asset that entrepreneurs can use to generate revenue and thus support economic growth. Crowdfunding is making waves and pumping bloodline which is money, to the reach of many entrepreneurs, philanthropists, communities and business organizations. Anyone and any group of people can seek for fund from the crowd. The limit for the use of crowdfunding is only set by the attractiveness of an idea and the way in which the idea is presented to the crowd.

The process of securing finance from the crowd relies heavily on ability of the project owner to elicit massive support from a sufficient group of potential contributors. It cannot work out without the support of the crowd. The crowd must connect to the reason behind the objective because crowdfunding is not an opportunity to ask for handouts. People connect with projects that they can see its bigger picture and the power behind the force.

The internet and social media has added wings of flight to crowdfunding activities. News of a new idea on a crowdfunding portal can literally be disseminated to millions of internet users within seconds. Several social media channels like websites, Blogs, Forums, FaceBook, Twitter, LinkedIn and YouTube has been used to establish connections and enhance emotional attachment.

Due to the global nature of most crowdfunding campaigns, it is important to present it in a way that the crowd can connect with it in a lease three different ways. The crowd wants to be able to connect with the main purpose of asking for funds, the reward attached to making a contribution and the creative display about the campaign. The creative display in reference here is video.

Who can use crowdfunding?

Crowdfunding has been used very successfully by small, medium and large businesses. It is not only small businesses and entrepreneurs that have the need for venture funds. Difficulties in obtaining business capital are an ailment that plagues businesses of different categories.

The only difference is that established business are more likely to get funds from mainstream financial institutions because they have been around and can supply all the evidences that lending institutions will require before they can lend. However it is noted that small businesses and entrepreneurs are more likely to use the option of crowdfunding because they have more opportunities to raise funds from the crowd than from traditional finance organizations.

One of the greatest challenges of business startups is the ability to source funds. Medium and large organizations are known to have used crowdfunding successfully in the areas of expanding their product re-launch and improve their brand.

Glyncoch Community Centre

Local communities are not left out of the crowdfunding space and its many inherent benefits. Glyncoch Community Centre, South Wales, United Kingdom launched a successful campaign for re-development of the community Centre. The Community had made several efforts to raise funds that will enable it carry out developmental works on its community

Centre. They were successful to an extent but they still could not raise the exact amount required to start the project. The community decided to go the way of crowdfunding. The campaign was successful and they were able to raise the final amount of £40,000 required to start the project.

The campaign had support from celebrities and corporate bodies like Deloitte, ASDA, and Wales and West Utilities and Tesco. The community wanted it and they got it through crowdfunding. Glyncoch Community Centre campaign was launched on spacehive.com

Nevaeh Belker

Even children are not left out of what is happening in crowdfunding. This is a very emotional story of an 11 year old that launched a crowdfunding campaign for a 6 years old friend called Nevaeh Belker. The 6 years old child was diagnosed with a brain tumor. He has had a surgery and was undergoing through chemotherapy. Through the campaign an amount was raised to help the boy's parents to settle some of the medical bills.

The LIFX Smartbulb

The LIFX smartbulb is a good example of where inventors do not have to become business strategists before they can succeed in their endeavors. These group of techies used the Kickstarter crowdfunding platform to pitch a campaign to raisc funds that will enable them develop a WIFI enabled bulb that is energy efficient. The project was to raise $100,000 but they got a pledge of $1,312,525 within five days. The group had to place a lid on receiving further pledges. This is really incredible. The crowd decides what they want, and they contribute to make it happen.

Ali Ganjavian: Ostrich pillow

This is one of the most successful projects so far in the era of crowdfunding. It is a simple but unique innovation about a travel pillow. The Ostrich pillow is an object that anyone can pull over the head to take a nap while travelling around. The owners have absolutely no idea it could become a sensation. Large department stores that otherwise would not have considered funding the production of such a weird looking pillow are now stocking it in large numbers.

Benefits of crowdfunding to the business community

Diversified portfolio

Crowdfunding brings the opportunity to have a diversified portfolio. In a crowdfunding project, an investor has the opportunity to spread a small amount of money into several projects.

This is especially important when it comes to the issue of spreading risk. It is easy to get into the business of lending and investing because it requires small amount of money to start investing.

Gain direct access to diverse investors

For many businesses that have a crowdfunding project, it can be an opportunity to have direct access to diverse groups of investors. Each investor group is more likely to bring with it a unique insight and proposition that could help a business.

Individuals and organizations are no more limited by their geographical location. Any one or a group of people can pitch a campaign and get support from several people across the globe.

Economic growth

It is a known fact that small businesses contribute largely to reduce unemployment by hiring locals in their area of operation. The ability to have easy access to finance needed for business start-ups and new business development is likely to create employment opportunities when those start-ups go into operation.

Why you need crowdfunding

Easy access to capital

Capital is one of the most difficult and scarce resource needed for achievement and fulfillment of several objectives. The need for capital is not limited to startups and entrepreneurs. Every venture will require some form of capital, be it for profit or not for profit.

Traditional sources of capital like banks, brokers and business angels have very strict requirement that many business startups cannot meet. Their systems are set up in such a way that they need to see compelling evidence of ability of repay back the loan or equity.

Seeking for funds from the crowd will in most cases not require any such evidence. The crowd will only need to have an emotional connection to the campaign objective. Traditional lending organizations may sometimes impose high interest rates that can land the startup into debt. In order cases like the case of business angels, an entrepreneur may even loose out by releasing too much equity.

Ability to test the market
Starting up a business can be very challenging. Even when an entrepreneur has the required fund to start a business, there is still need to test

the market for validation of product, service or idea. Crowdfunding campaign can serve as a tool for market validation.

An entrepreneur will be able to find out if the product or service is acceptable to target market or not. Due to the diverse nature of the crowd, the entrepreneur is able to make some corrections or re-draft a business strategy as a result of comments from the crowd. In traditional lending circles, the question of proof of concept is always a challenge for many business startups. The process of crowdfunding tends to bridge that gap for many entrepreneurs by creating opportunities for market validation.

Alternative marketing tool

Many crowdfunding platforms incorporate the use of online communities to generate contributions or donations for individual projects. In that same way, campaigns get high visibility from such online exposures. Even visitors to the crowdfunding portal that do not have money to contribute may decide to help with creating an online buzz for a campaign.

Any well designed campaign may likely get links from several thousands of website visitors who were directed either through a link or from a social network. Indiegogo has become the first crowdfunding platform to allow campaigners to embed their project page into another website or Blog. This new development will help to deepen the market of crowdfunding and foster economic growth across the globe.

Gain potential loyal customers

A crowdfunding campaign is likely to generate attention from the crowd. There are likely to be comments, questions, feedback or ideas from people who have viewed or read the campaign.

This will give the campaigner an opportunity to fine tune business ideas.

Potential customers who have genuine interest in the product or service are likely to help the campaign to straighten our grey areas about the business idea. The way a campaign responds to comment and questions are likely to endear potential customers who may become early adopters. In most cases, early adopters help the business to build a brand, advertise the business by sending referral and may be customers for a long time.

The risks

Crowdfunding is packed full of notable opportunities that is available for anyone with a good idea. However it is not without a second side of the coin like all other aspects of life. Due to the fact that many business startups are set up by untested hands in the area of business or management of projects, there is no guarantee that the business or the project will succeed. If a project or the business did not succeed, investors may not receive a return on their investment.

A failure of that business or the project could even result to total loss of both capital and the expected return on the capital. Another aspect of the risk may not be in the aspect of losing funds that were invested into the business, it could result to a loss of control where more shares are issued by the business. If more shares are issued unexpectedly, the investment could be diluted. In some circumstances, it may take a longer time for a startup business to generate a good return. In such a situation, the investor may have to wait for longer time before a return on the investment can be due.

How to protect yourself

It is always imperative that an investor should investigate and analyze any investment before parting with money. In other types of investments due diligence is required on the part of the investor. It should not be different when investing in crowdfunding projects.

As an investor, or even a donor, make sure you have a good understanding of the business and its process. If you cannot do that yourself, get a professional investment advisor to help you out. One of the questions you might need to ask will be the likely time to expect return on your investment. Important information you need to know before you invest will be to find out if the business has any form of insurance protection.

Size of crowdfunding market and its growth patterns

Crowdfunding market came like a bomb and it is spreading all over the internet with diverse target markets. Though the concept has been around for centuries, the internet and social media brought the explosion. It is relatively new and the data surrounding that growth is still sparsely distributed. Nonetheless experts are making predictions about the likely market size. Deloitte predicted that crowdfunding will raise US$3 billion in 2013. Another prediction from Massolutions is that crowdfunding will raise about US$5 billion in 2013.

The future of crowdfunding is very bright by my estimation. The market is still evolving and will continue to evolve. It is not planning to settle because exotic ideas are emerging daily. The World Bank also predicted that crowdfunding may become a key funding source for the developing world. The Bank further predicted that crowdfunding has the potential to reach $93 billion per annum in developing countries by 2025

This prediction is made despite the fact that crowdfunding in the era of social media and internet is virtually unknown or unheard of in many developing countries despite its exponential growth in many developed countries. If the prediction by the World Bank becomes a reality, it means that crowdfunding market may have a wider depth than expected by many observers.

Chapter 2

Crowdfunding investment opportunities

The concept of social lending and giving is getting more popular by the day. In the year 2013, significant progress were made both in the technology of social lending and giving called crowdfunding, and in the types of projects that were pitched for funding from crowdfunding platforms. Crowdfunding provides an exciting opportunity for investors who want to do something different from the traditional way of investment. Investment in crowdfunding can be for profit or not for profit. This chapter is dedicated to the discussion on investments for profit in a crowdfunding project.

It is thought by industry observers that crowdfunding investors provide loans to borrower and the business community at a rate and condition that is friendlier than those offered by traditional lending organizations like banks and angel investors. There are many exciting opportunities to be part of the new way of funding projects and businesses. Opportunities are there for everyone that wants to be part of it.

Potential investors need to understand the dynamics and mechanics of crowdfunding. Investors are advised to dig a little deeper to identify and understand the business and projects to pair and partner with while still being profitable. Investment experts warn that investing in early stage business or startups could be risky. Investors are to take due diligence to mitigate the risk of loss.

How crowdfunding investment works

Investment in a crowdfunding project could be either for equity stake in the company or for an interest on capital. In an equity crowdfunding investment, the investor will receive an equity holding in the company. Investors get a return on their investment when the company pays a dividend, if the company is sold or listed on a stock exchange.

Equity investments in crowdfunding circle are in most cases used by startup companies that are looking for funds to start their business. In a peer to peer lending investment, investors have the opportunity to lend directly to members while avoiding the complexity of the traditional banking system. The savings on interest and rates are shared by both the borrower and lender. At the end of it, the borrowers get better rates and lenders get better returns on their investment. Peer to peer lending platforms play the role of providing a better space for lenders and borrowers to transact.

Why people invest in crowdfunding

The decision to invest in a crowdfunding project or business has been found to be motivated by several factors. Some of these include the expected return on investment, emotional sentiments attached to some projects, desire to support friends and family, the pride of being part of success story and the idea of being a co-partner in progress.

Many industry observers have projected that social lending provides higher returns on investments and borrowers get a lower interest rates on loans than the rates offered by banks. The dynamics of crowdfunding investment is easy for many people to understand and a lot of potential investors are embracing that opportunity to get higher returns while avoiding the complexity of traditional bank investment.

There is never a better time to invest in crowdfunding than now. This is because opportunities that were left to the selected few are at the fingertips of every one. Another interesting aspect of crowdfunding investment is that the investor can become an active participant in every aspects of the business. In traditional investment circles, the investor plays a passive role in management of the company.

Potentials of crowdfunding investment

Wider market reach

In the world of traditional investment, the options are narrower than in a crowdfunding investment. This is because the reach of internet made it possible for anyone to investment in any geographical location without having a physical presence in that location. The use of social networks to advertise crowdfunding projects has expanded crowdfunding investment opportunities to a much wider reach than traditional investment opportunities can ever have. The borrower that is struggling to get loans from traditional lenders has an expanded opportunity, as well as the potential lender who wants to start playing in the investment market.

Opportunity to diversify investments at low cost

Crowdfunding offers potential investors the opportunities to invest very small amounts that can be as low as $20 or £10. It thus means that any potential investor can start small and grow a diverse portfolio of investments without spending a huge sum of money on each. On CrowdCube crowdfunding platform, equity investments can start as low as £10. Diversification of investment helps with mitigating investment risk. An investor who can spread the risks may not lose all investments if there is default in any company.

Know your business associate

Know your customers (KYC) is a normal aspect of business due diligence. An investor in crowdfunding has better options of investigating to know the potential borrower. The internet is wide and open. Investors can carry out extensive research and inquiries into the life and business activities of borrowers.

Potential investors have the opportunity to ask open questions to borrowers. Even some borrowers pre-empt some expected questions that a potential investor may want to ask, and they supply answers to such questions in form of Frequently Asked Questions (FAQ). The borrower can also make an informed decision about the sentiments and personality of the lender, thereby setting out plans to meet requirements of the lender. The dynamics of crowdfunding investment makes it easy and efficient for screening of investors, borrowers and lenders. There is increased transparency and data accuracy due to wide range of internet technologies.

Tax breaks

In some countries the government has stepped up to support investment in crowdfunding by setting some tax benefits for crowdfunding investors. In the United Kingdom, Seed Enterprise Investment Scheme (SEIS) and Enterprise Investment Scheme (EIS) is one such support. It is a scheme that allows startups to register under its umbrella. Investors that invest in a startup company registered under the scheme can claim up to 50% of original investment off income tax.

In the event of failure of a SEIS registered company, the investor may be able to make some claims. If the business succeeds and start paying dividend, the investor may also claim on capital gains tax. This is an absolute win-win situation.

Chapter 3

Crowdfunding – How it all started

Crowdfunding is no doubt a buzz word on the internet in recent times, but it is not a new concept or phenomenon. It is an age long idea that has been in use hundreds of years ago. Even in the recent past, crowdfunding idea has continued to play major part in developmental projects around the world. It is in history that many public buildings and statues were funded through crowdfunding effort. What has made crowdfunding to become a buzz word is the combination of the effective and efficient use of internet technologies. The complex interactions of activities of the web 2.0 brought crowdfunding into the limelight.

Social media has made human interaction over the web an easy and enjoyable activity. Connection with people any time anywhere irrespective of their geographical location has greatly facilitated the ease of soliciting for support on any type of project. Online communities have become an order of the day. Anyone can join any online community or even start a new one to meet the need of likeminded people and organizations. Finding people with special interest and passion to support a given project has become an easy task unlike when such interaction is limited to specific geographic location. The internet has given crowdfunding a new wing of flight.

Crowdfunding has a long history that dates back to the 1700's. History has it that Irish Loan Fund started by Jonathan Swift in the 1700s, was used to provide and facilitate micro loans to poor families in the rural areas. It was reported to have provided more than 300 hundred families with the opportunity to start a new business. The novelty lies in the technologies and the mindset that are giving it a new momentum. Technologies and mindset that will be considered in this chapter is the chronological record of the main events leading to what we now refer to as crowdfunding.

Crowdfunding at the inception of the internet

The internet gave the concept of crowdfunding a new impetus because of the ease of connection of people with related interest though they may scattered in different geographic areas. One of the earlier public uses of the internet to solicit for help to fund a project was recorded in 1997. It was a reunion tour project that a British Rock Band called Marillion, funded by online donations from their fans. The band was reported as having raised $60,000 from that crowdfunding project. At that time there were no crowdfunding platforms, so the project was managed by fans.

A film industry director Mark Tapio Kines was able to raise $125,000 between 1997 and 1999 to fund a film project. This innovative way of funding a project made waves and started generating ideas and arguments that resulted to crowdfunding as we know it today.

The millennium and crowdfunding

ArtistShare is the first notable crowdfunding platform that sprang up in year 2000 as a result of the inspiration of the Rock Band. Other forms of fund raising activities that could be regarded as crowdfunding gradually began to emerge. Another example of the earlier platform in 2000 is JustGiving.com. As the millennium progressed, another twist of raising funds from the public emerged with the launching of KIVA. This is purely a micro lending platform that allows investors to lend money to individuals in developing countries, to enable them set up businesses. Though the concept is not entirely the same as crowdfunding, it has many related features because it includes all the social network features of current crowdfunding platforms.

The revolution of soliciting for help from crowds through the internet kept on growing and in 2004, a band called Electric Eel Shock, raised £10,000 from 100 fans to enable them take a tour. A crowd donation system created by Franny Armstrong in 2004 lasted about five years from June 2004 to June 2009, and she was able to raise £1,500,000. Still in 2004, Benjamin Pommeraud and Guillaume Colboc who are film producers launched their crowd donation campaign and they were able to raise $50,000. The fund was raised to fund their short science fiction film, Demain la Veille.

The re-birth of online funds collection

By 2006, crowdfunding was beginning to take another twist due to the growth of the social web. It has been widely reported on the internet that the current name given to soliciting for help from diverse group of people using the internet was coined by Michael Sullivan. He was purported to have coined the term "Crowdfunding" when he was describing the process of raising money online for video projects. The term crowdfunding did not catch up fast until 2008 and 2009 when the likes of Indiegogo and KickStarter entered the crowdfunding market

SellaBand became the first platform to use the model and to set up a platform for musicians to enable them raise funds to record an album. Year 2007 came with the birth of another popular micro lending platform called LendingClub. But social networks in those years were similar to operating system. It was more only about becoming friend with someone or live-chatting. At this time, social networks were becoming platforms with ability to support a broad range of social applications and interactive functionalities. However, identities and experiences were still essentially disconnected between them.

Crowdfunding and the social networks

The exponential growth in the number of projects funded through crowdfunding platforms could not have been achieved without very strong connection in the reach and power of social engagements in social media. All through the ages, crowds do form and connect in circles designed for special interests. But the power of such affinity has always been limited by geographical boundaries. The internet and social media broke down such barriers and let loose the social nature of man. The duo released the bottled up passion and need to support others and get involved with people and organizations in a way to improve, create and innovate circumstances and situations.

The founders of IndieGoGo, Danae Ringelmann and Slava Rubin were quoted as saying that they started the company to "democratize fundraising" and "to empower creative entrepreneurs with Do-It-With-Others (DIWO) tools." Though the duo had different educational and career backgrounds, they had one thing in common. And that was to provide room for alternative funding.

The passion to help others find funding from non traditional sources was borne from their various experiences of not been able to raise finance for their ventures. When they launched Indiegogo in 2008, they started with the film industry. Due to the astonishing success they had with the film industry they were motivated to open up their platform for all other industries.

By 2009 Kickstarter was launched with the philosophy of "new way to fund creativity" by Perry Chen, Yancey Strickler, and Charles Adler. From this point crowdfunding started emerging in a new way. They are open to various industries and have funded various projects ranging from films, music, journalism and even food related industries. Kickstarter helped to enforce the use of the new term for "crowdfunding,"

Prosper and LendingClub also came onto the crowdfunding scene in 2009. Their motivation is to establish direct connection of lenders and borrowers through the internet. The sudden influx of various social networks was the main reason why crowdfunding started gathering momentum. Individuals and organizations were using the networks to spread the good news about crowdfunding platforms and the projects that were being funded through them.

Technological infrastructure and social sharing mindset has set up online relationships of various degrees at this time. Sharing of social information was beginning to go viral, and that became the fertilizer that crowdfunding needed to thrive.

By 2010, the exciting growth of the number of projects funded through crowdfunding platforms became very infectious. More people were signing on to various social networks and more social network platforms were hitting the newsstands every day. That excitement set some creative minds into action and the year saw the birth of yet another flavor of crowdfunding. The GrowCV was set up to be an equity based crowdfunding platform.

Up till the year 2010, there were no known equity only crowdfunding platform. It was a concept that came just in time. Venture Capitalists were beginning to feel left out of the excitement. They wanted to be part of the crowd that are shaping destinies and the future of business finance. Even non venture capitalists that have the dream to become venture capitalist, but lacked the necessary financial muscle saw the birth of GrowVC as a very welcoming change.

The operation of GrowVC is more like that of KIVA except that it was focused on technology startups and positions itself to help startups secure initial funding of up to $1M. While the dust is yet to settle Crowdcube came onto the scene in 2011 and announced itself as the world's first business finance crowdfunding platform for businesses to raise equity funds. From this point on, several crowdfunding platforms have been set up to help entrepreneurs, small businesses and other existing business to fund and grow their business through rewards and equity crowdfunding

Crowdfunding has come of age

While the crowdfunding market was getting all the attention of the press and the entire internet community, various state governments of the world were watching with interest. The government of the United States of America was one of the first to show a positive support for crowdfunding. It realized that crowdfunding is not a force to be ignored because it was beginning to revolutionalize the business scene for business startups. In 2011, crowdfunding gained the necessary support it needs to thrive, and in 2012, President Barack Obama gave it the final approval. The Jumpstart Our Business Startups (JOBS) Act was signed into law.

The best part of the JOBS act came in 2013 when Securities and Exchange Commission (SEC) lifted ban on publicizing shares in private offerings. In the past it was extremely difficult for small companies and entrepreneurs to raise money because of the ban on the advertising of such activity. With the lifting of the ban, companies can now advertise their private placement memorandum on Twitter, YouTube, Facebook, and all other social media platforms. Private placement memorandum can also be advertised through press.

Chapter 4

How Crowdfunding works

Crowdfunding platforms use the support and power of the crowd to fund various types of projects with different types of business models. These crowdfunding platforms has emerged over the years to enable the process of raising funds from diverse and geographically located people through the internet. They are specialist in the process of organizing crowdfunding activities. In recent times, many state governments are beginning to consider how to regulate activities of crowdfunding platforms due to their economic importance.

At any point in time, there are several hundreds of thousands of people that need funding for different types of projects. Though crowdfunding is creating a buzz, the number of people requiring funding makes it imperative that anyone or organization that wants to benefit from that market will need to have a very clear and sharp objective.

Make your objective worth the investment

Though the money will come from the crowd, you need to know that any donation has an impact on someone's finances. Therefore the objective has to be clearly specified in a way that people can identify with it.

The crowd will be happy to identify with an objective that can show an in-depth research before a pitch is submitted to a crowdfunding platform. Though an in-depth research is required, the pitch is expected to be presented in a simple and plain style language.

Your ability to engage the crowd with your pitch will determine whether it will be successful or not. The crowd will buy your personality and passion as well as your idea. The level of engagement required to engage with the crowd can be very involving and intensive. There are likely to be questions from the crowd, and you are required to provide answers to those questions. It is only normal for potential donors and investors to want to get clarifications on certain issues that may affect the project outcome.

Transparency is the starting point

Transparency is required all the way. As the questions are posed to you, make your answers to be very clear and unambiguous. The need to be open with disclosure of issues cannot be over emphasized. My advice is to preempt possible questions from potential investors. As you prepare to launch a campaign, also prepare possible questions and answers for the crowd.

Even if the crowdfunding project did not meet your expected objective, the questions from the crowd would have helped you to examine your objective through the microscope of the crowd. The end product will definitely help you to make your idea a better one.

Recently, a crowdfunding project went sour when the crowd discovered that the person seeking funds from the crowd can actually afford to raise the funds without recourse to the crowd. The actions from the crowd immediately turned to a negative one. There was a story of a 9 years old girl Mackenzie Wilson, who wanted to learn how to build a video game. She needed to attend a Science, Technology, Engineering and Mathematics (STEM) camp to learn before she can embark on building the game. She implored her mum who agreed and helped her to launch a campaign on Kickstarter crowdfunding platform. The story was very inspirational and the campaign was able to raise about $20,000 in a short time though her original goal was for $829. The campaign attracted many positive comments and contribution because the crowd was able to identify with her objective. Others wanted to support the girl child to do something very creative.

However, just as the crowd were excited to support her ambition, they were easily offended by what they called lack of transparency. It was discovered that the girl's mother is a successful entrepreneur.

The girl's mother was quoted as saying that she did not launch the campaign with the intention to defraud, but rather as a way to encourage the girl to raise the money she needed for her venture. Whether it is really a case of misrepresentation is a subject for further discussion. This is because there were people among the crowd that did not agree that it was a lack of transparency issue.

There are no sign posts at the crowdfunding platforms to indicate that the funds from the crowd are for people who cannot afford to raise required funds. Yet, the crowd reacted in a negative way when they found out that the person making the pitch can actually raise the funds from personal saving. In effect, transparency has to be the only option because you can lose all support if the crowd has any reason to think that what you presented is not exactly as it is. Support from the crowd has to be earned before you can succeed in a crowdfunding activity.

What investors see in a project

Some investors can tell you that they could not point at what moved them to show support for a particular project. Sometimes it could be the personality of the project owner, while some investors will tell you that it is the way the project was presented. This is why I will advise anyone that wants to seek fund from the crowd to be very original in the presentation. No one project will attract the interest of everyone. But if you believe in what you are saying, show it by your actions.

Investors in crowdfunding projects have various reasons and motivations that drive their decision to invest in any given project. Motivations range from emotional, personal and business. Emotional motivations could be traced to people that wants to support certain industry or certain activities due to some non-economic reasons. Another motivator for investors in crowdfunding projects is their perception of the market potential of the product or service. Business investors are usually not emotional in their approach to making investment decisions. Their decisions are based on their analysis of the market potential of the product or service.

In most cases, seasoned investors will easily get attracted to products or service that is in tune with their usual type of investment. Other investors will only invest on projects that were presented by people or organizations that have a track record in a certain industry or market. These types of investors are not driven by emotional reasons. They are usually those that will invest purely for economic reasons. Investors that invest on experienced organizations are usually risk conscious and will want to deal with historical facts about good performance in the past.

Crowdfunding models

Though there is a buzz about this new kid on the block called crowdfunding, it is still a new and developing sector. It is almost magical and exciting, but potential participants can easily be confused because of the various flavors in which it is presented. As the crowdfunding market heats up, various models are being adopted. It is still at an experimental stage. Several countries are still trying to figure out how to deal with this new phenomenon called crowdfunding. Thus, there are little or no regulations in most countries to deal with crowdfunding.

As a new sector, it is still in the works but there are four models that have clearly emerged. It may change in the future but at this point in time, the models are those that are for donation, reward, debts and equity.

Donation model

Crowdfunding platforms that operate under this model use the philanthropic procedures. Donors are not allowed to have financial interest in projects, however they do feel that they have sense of ownership. This is a situation where people have an emotional connection and believe strongly in the cause that the project is trying to support or promote.

Justgiving.com is a typical example of a donation based crowdfunding platform. It provides necessary tools and services to enable donors to give and to support their favorite charities and projects. The company also provides the platform that enables fund raisers to pitch their campaign to the right crowd. This model also has a flavor to give back something that is not measured in economic terms. These can be acknowledgements, free gifts, or a mention on publications. Using this model, project owners can acknowledge certain category of donors. Other categories may receive free gifts. It is left for the project owner to get creative with the way the categories are defined.

Debt model

As the word suggests, debt means that the contributions are just loans that will be repaid at a future date. Investors are assured that they will receive back their principal plus interest or without interest amount, depending on the terms and conditions of the loan. This model is often used in a peer-to-peer lending environment. In this situation, the investor will receive the money back irrespective of whether the business declares a profit or not.

In as much as investors get their money back with interest, they also see it as an opportunity to support businesses that may not ordinarily be able to get loans from traditional banks. Some peer to peer lending platforms allow investors to lend money without requesting for interest. What the investor will get back at the end of the term is the principal amount. It has been noted that some debt crowdfunding platform use credit scoring to assess borrowers.

Fundingcircle.com is a crowdfunding platform that facilitates peer to peer lending. It has made it possible for almost anyone to be able to lend money for projects of interest. It is interesting to note that even the UK government is lending money to businesses and individuals through the FundingCircle platform. With the operation of peer to peer lending platforms, small businesses are getting the funds they need for their business while individuals and business organizations are getting good returns for their investments. I call this a win-win situation.

Equity model

In equity based crowdfunding, investors are regarded as shareholders in the business or the projects. This is situation where investors are paid dividend only when the business declares a profit. From the entrepreneurs' point of view, it is another opportunity to do business like the big companies without the structures and framework of big companies. Any small business, irrespective of the industry can now be able to pitch to the crowd to meet its need for funding.

Success with this model of crowdfunding will require the business that requires fund to exhibit an ability to effectively recruit potential investors who share the same passion and may want to support their business. The ability to create a persuasive pitch may be the starting point but a strategy to manage large numbers of small investors is what will determine how well the business will perform.

A good example of am crowdfunding platform operating this model is Seedrs. It is an equity based crowdfunding platform that allows micro investors to invest in companies though their online platform. Using the Seedrs platform, investors can invest as little as £10 in any company registered on the platform. Seedrs operates the 'all or nothing' principle where projects on the platform must meet its target. If the project could not meet its target, the project owner will not receive any fund, and all pledged funds are returned to the backers. The need to develop equity-based crowdfunding marketing strategy cannot be over emphasized.

This is because investors in this category are a bit different from the other investors in other models of crowdfunding. The investors are usually business savvy and profit oriented people who wants a good return on their investment. They are more likely to research about a business online before they make a financial commitment.

Reward model

This model of crowdfunding has since been the most popular type of crowdfunding platform. This model has been successfully used for funding of several types of projects including social and entrepreneurial projects.

Using this model, contributors are promised a non-financial reward in return for their support. The support could be monetary or non-monetary. Kickstarter – a crowdfunding platform has successfully used this model. Since it is a non -financial reward, Kickstarter always advise project backers to use their good judgment before backing a project. Project owners have the responsibility to fulfill reward promises.

Chapter 5

Challenges of crowdfunding

The prospect of investing in crowdfunding is no doubt very attractive and appealing. It can be a very rewarding experience to invest in startups and early stage companies. This can only happen if you can identify a good startup before it becomes a sensation to the general public. There is another side of the picture that this chapter will paint for you. It is not intended to scare you or cause you to panic. The intention is give you a balanced view of crowdfunding that will surely help you to make informed decision if you need to venture into the world of crowdfunding.

It is well known fact in investment circles that investment in early stage companies or startups are risky despite the potential gains. There is every possibility that the business may not take off. Even when it takes off on schedule, it may not withstand the initial storms of business cycle. The implication is that you might lose all your investments. It is widely speculated that 50% of new companies fail within the first year. It is therefore very important to have an investment strategy that will help you identify your investment psychology. If you are a risk averse investor, then you may need to rethink if crowdfunding is your type of game. If your risk appetite is good and you have the capacity to tolerate volatility and instability in small caps investment, then go for it. In all situations, you will need a solid business plans to map out your investments route. It has been established that repayments of micro loans tend to be higher than repayments of loans from traditional lending sector. There may be some false notions that crowdfunding means getting easy money for any untested business. Undiscerning investors also think that making money through social lending is as free as breeze. It is not exactly so.

Crowdfunding is not an all comers' game. It requires a lot of work, and there is no guarantee that all efforts may amount to anything tangible or even success. It is not a get rich quick scheme, neither is it an ad-hoc funding arrangement. In some circles, some people are touting the impression that anyone with a supposedly great idea can throw it at crowdfunding platforms and before you can click the Submit button on your computer, donors and investors are already falling over the offer. While that may have happened in few cases, it is hardly a general experience.

Issues to consider before making a crowdfunding investment

Potential risk of investment

Startup businesses are in most cases managed or promoted by people who may not have tried to manage a business. In some cases the business may be a brain child of an idealist or an enthusiast. The idea may look very good on paper but because it has not been tried, no one knows for sure how it will fare in practice. The same goes for early stage businesses. An investor in startup and early stage business should understand that the managers of the business may still be learning the twists and turns of the road to business success. The high volatility in paddling the boat of startups is the risk of investing in startups. While the owners or managers are learning the curves, the boat may capsize.

When it capsizes, all may be lost. If all is not lost, it may take some time to repair the boat with the implication that arrival to destination port will be delayed. That delay could result to a delay in business profitability and payment of dividends. It is therefore important to invest only in what you can afford to lose in any one company. Another option is to have a well defined plan to diversify your portfolio.

Liquidity risk

The ease at which you can get in and out of investment purchase agreement is an important aspect of business. Crowdfunding equity investments are not likely to be very liquid. Small cap stocks are not easily marketable. In the case of crowdfunding, it may even be more difficult to offload the shares.

This is because the shares are not listed on any stock exchange. It may still happen but it has not happened yet. Crowdfunding investment market is not liquid. This is why it is risky and may affect your total wellbeing. It is important to note that history has recorded many financially affluent individuals who had to go into bankruptcy because they could not manage their financial liquidity. If you cannot hold the stock for a long time or even wait for the company to turn over profit and start paying dividend, it means that crowdfunding investment is not for you. An example is that in the United States of America, under the JOBS Act, a crowdfunding investment is subject to a minimum of 12 months contract. In peer to peer lending, the debts are not easily transferable. If you finance a business under a debt agreement, and you suddenly need to callback your cash, you may not be able to easily sell the debt to another financier.

Dividend may or may not be

Dividend payments are made by a business to its shareholders after a successful trading year. Many startups may not be able to pay dividends in the first one or two years of trading. Inability to pay dividends is not a special problem for startups or early stage businesses. In some cases even well established businesses are not able to pay dividend for some reasons related to poor performance. However an investor needs to be aware of the possibility of not receiving dividend or any form of return on investment in the early years of the business. It may be more distressing if the stock is not listed on any stock exchange because that will make transferability more difficult. In most cases, except where it is pre-offered, businesses are not obliged to pay dividend every year.

Dilution of investment

Any investment may be diluted if the investor did not invest in further shares when the company issues more shares. Dilution of investment is not an issue that primarily affects startups or early stage businesses. It can occur in any equity investment. Dilution may not be a problem for an investor that owns a very small percentage of stakes in a company.

An investor who owns a large number of shares, and who is ultimately nursing an ambition to wield strong influence in the affairs of the business may not be favorably disposed if there is dilution of the stakes. This is especially true for investors that want to influence decisions using their voting rights. The investor can mitigate against the risk of dissolution by exercising the right that most businesses extend to their shareholders. That right is the right of pre-emption. A pre-emption right under company shareholding agreement is a right of first option to buy. This means that even if the company issues more shares, existing shareholders are given the opportunity to acquire more shares before it is offered to the public.

It is important to ensure that pre-emption right is included in any contractual agreement for an equity investment. Though pre-emption right is obligatory on the company if it is included in the contract agreement, it is not obligatory for the shareholder to exercise that right of option to acquire more stakes in a company. Inclusion of pre-emption right agreement is a statutory requirement in some countries while it is not so in many countries. Be an informed investor and protect yourself from the challenges of equity investment dilution by always ensuring that a right of pre-emption is included in equity investments of your choice.

Risk of fraud

The risk of fraud on internet based transactions cannot be over emphasized. Internet is ubiquitous in nature and the reach is wider than traditional business arena. It is very easy and comfortable to transact business over the internet. It is in fact as easy as clicking a button. Thus it is the same ease through which fraudsters can defraud undiscerning internet users.

There are many fraudsters perpetuating their fraudulent and unethical activities using the hood of the internet. It is of note that crowdfunding is likely to appeal to unsophisticated investors. Some of these investors are those that were not able to participate in mainstream investment markets. They may not have the knowledge and experience to investigate and determine if an investment is real or if it is a fraud waiting to happen. This makes these classes of investors to be more vulnerable to fraudsters.

Most potentially fraudulent investments are full of fantastic offers and promises. Sometimes they sound too good to be true. A discerning investor can actually see that some investment offers are designed for fraud. There are some cases where genuine investment offers turned to fraud due to unwholesome business process. Many legitimate investment offers became fraudulent offers because promoters or the managers did not institute a fraud proof business process that can help to mitigate risk. Investors with get rich quick mindset are more likely to fall into the pit of fraudsters. Such investors may fail to investigate and analyze an investment offer before investing into it.

Unfortunately in some cases, a legitimate and genuine investment offer can still become risky. This could happen in a situation where promoters or the business managers have no intention to use the investment for the intended purpose. This is a big challenge but industry regulators and crowdfunding platforms can help to prevent this type of risk by instituting clear process of monitoring funded projects to ensure compliance.

Entrepreneurial risk

Entrepreneurs are not left out of the challenges of crowdfunding. When an entrepreneur decides to use crowdfunding platforms to raise the much needed business finance, there are concerns about the safety of ideas, concepts and business plan. One of the major concern is that entrepreneur may lose the idea or concept to better-funded businesses.

A concept or idea could be stolen and patented before the original owner can recognize that the concept has been copied. Also for same reason of lack of funds, a stolen idea or concept may not be easily recovered due to high cost of litigation that may be required. In traditional funding circles, an entrepreneur can insist that potential funders must sign an agreement of non-disclosure. But the nature of the internet and the mechanics of crowdfunding make it very cumbersome to request that anyone who wants to access the project page must sign a non-disclosure agreement.

The other side of the coin is that investors also run the risk of investing in stolen concepts or ideas. When an investment is made on such shaky business venture, a resultant law suit may wipe out all the finance invested in the business thereby rendering return on investment to become zero.

Legal risk

A typical concern for legal matters on crowdfunding investment is that of perception of offers, absence of standard reporting standards and lack of clear standards on entry and exit from investment. Many countries are still struggling on how to incorporate crowdfunding concept into the financial mechanism of the state.

This situation has exposed so many unsophisticated investors to the danger of not being able to interpret the meanings of some complex crowdfunding initiatives. As a new and growing phenomenon, there are still many greys areas that even state governments have not been able to demystify. Investors may have to be careful about investing in a very long circle projects. This is because state governments may eventually come up with rules that may turn earlier legal agreements to illegality.

Poor stock valuation

There are notable concerns among traditional investment communities, stating that some of the equity investments on crowdfunding platforms have unrealistic valuations. Crowdfunding relies on the wisdom of the crowd to determine what they are willing to spend on, and how much they want to spend on it. However, investment industry players are beginning to raise some concerns about reliance on wisdom of the crowd to valuate stocks. The crowd in most cases is not financial experts.

Many of the people among the crowd are not tutored in the school of equity valuation. Their perception on equity valuation may not be in line with what industry experts expect it to be. The implication is that both the investor and the entrepreneur may run the risk of either having an over-valued or under-valued stock.

If the stock price is overvalued, the investor may not receive return on investment at the right time, while the entrepreneur will take a swap home. On the reverse side, if the stock value is undervalued, the entrepreneur may end up working for little or nothing and will not get any return on investment.

A crowdfunding platform has taken the step to create a meeting point by adopting an auction based approach where the interaction of market forces sets the value of an equity investment. Recent expression of interest in equity crowdfunding by business angels and other traditional financiers will largely help to surmount the challenges of stock valuation for crowdfunding equities.

Complexity of managing large number of shareholders

A typical equity investment in a crowdfunding platform may likely attract very large number of shareholders. This is not unrelated to the low investment amount required for an investor to participate in equity crowdfunding. Large and established businesses that employed several professionals to manage shareholders do still struggle with managing shareholders.

Most small businesses are not equipped with the infrastructure and human resources required to manage large number of shareholders. As part of the industry players' initiatives to confront and surmount some of the challenges facing crowdfunding, Seedrs – a crowdfunding platform, developed a nominee model. Under the nominee model, all the equities are held by a single entity – the nominee. The nominee model is made with the intention to protect investors and also the business.

Chapter 6

Crowdfunding platforms

As the exciting features of crowdfunding market unwind, different operating flavors are emerging. It is quite obvious that many more operating models will still emerge because the market is still new and the vast opportunities yet untapped. Crowdfunding activities thrive on the use of social networks. Today, many social networks are beginning to set up crowdfunding platforms that are specially geared to meet the needs of members.

The number of platforms for crowdfunding is growing daily and it is likely to continue to grow because, social communities are beginning to define their own specific crowdfunding platforms. The effect is that people crowdfunding projects in such networks are likely to gain attention of investors or donors.

Types of crowdfunding platforms

The models that are in the market as at the time of writing are Equity, Reward, Donation and Debt models. Debt model is also called Peer to Peer lending model. The reach of the internet and its inherent potential growth, wide spread of social networks and internet technologies, flurry of opportunities are exploding in a way to make crowdfunding more successful than ever.

Some crowdfunding platforms operate a single model. Platforms like FundedByMe, FundTheGap, CrowdCube, Gambitious and Invesdor operates purely on one model. The model is equity based model. While some platforms combine two or three models. Examples of platforms that combine up to two or three models are Fundable and Squareknot. As the market is still growing, I suppose that crowdfunding platforms are still experimenting to find the best fit while the market for crowdfunding is being shaped by the crowd.

Equity based crowdfunding platform

This model of crowdfunding recognizes the funder as a shareholder in the company. It has certain legal and constitutional restriction in the way it is conducted. Equity based crowdfunding model operates on a legal framework of equity capital. This is probably why it is still illegal in some countries. An investor to an equity based crowdfunding project will eventually become a shareholder and thus have a right to vote and to receive dividends when the company declares a profit. On the other side of the coin, if the company makes a loss or even fails to succeed in its venture, the investor may lose all invested capital. Potential investors are seeing this model as a great opportunity to be part of next big ideas while investing a small amount of money.

How equity based crowdfunding works

Due to strict legal requirement of this type of model, it is still not allowed in various countries. The laws regulating this model of crowdfunding vary from country to country. In countries where it is allowed, the platform is required to satisfy certain regulatory requirement. The platforms are usually required to register with constitutionally approved authorities who will manage the registration process. There are obvious reasons why such strict regulatory requirements are in place for platforms operating equity based crowdfunding model. It is not suitable for all companies. There is need for the state to verify those companies that are best designed to operate with such a model.

The number of investors in a company's project may be too many for a small company to manage. If such magnitude of investors and investment are not properly managed, it could lead to business failure, which may in turn lead to loss of investment. The state's owes it as a duty to its citizens to protect both the investor and the business from collapse and abuse. In most cases the organizations seeking for fund from the crowd are untested hands in their area of business. Thus the likelihood of fraud or mismanagement of fund is not remote. This is where regulatory authorities play the role of getting the business seeking a funding to clearly explain aspects of their offering like the terms and conditions, the risks and other useful information that can help potential investor to ascertain viability of the business.

Regulatory authorities are there to protect the investor by verifying all claims and disclosures, and also protect the organization by ensuring they did not make disclosure that can put their organization at risk. It is of interest to note that rookie investors could lose their money because they often may not understand the meaning of some risks even when they are clearly stated.

Equity based crowdfunding in the UK

In the United Kingdom (UK), The Financial Conduct Authority (FCA) is the regulatory body that oversees the operations of equity based crowdfunding platforms. Some of the equity crowdfunding platforms in the UK are Crowdcube, Seedrs and Squareknot. They are authorized to operate equity based crowdfunding model. The FCA is not regulating the business of other types of crowdfunding platforms, but there are indications that it may likely start regulating the activities of other models of crowdfunding platforms.

Equity crowdfunding in the United Kingdom is still focused on sophisticated investors at this time. There is no defined law for equity based crowdfunding platforms. The platforms are operating under exemptions put in place by the FCA. This is probably why equity crowdfunding is still considered a high risk venture. United Kingdom is still working at an equity based crowdfunding regulation.

Equity based crowdfunding in the USA

It was illegal to operate an equity based crowdfunding platform in the United States of America until the passing of The JOBS Act in April 2012. The JOBS Act stands for "Jumpstart Our Business Startups". The Securities and Exchange Commission (SEC) is the body that regulates and authorizes equity based crowdfunding platforms.

JOBS Act came as a palliative to help small companies to solicit business funds from the public. This was done by relaxing of some of the prohibitive regulatory requirements that can only be met by big businesses. The Act provides an avenue for micro investors to invest in start-up companies. Recent economic recession succeeded in drying up investable funds from banks. Small businesses and business start-ups are finding it very difficult to get funds for their business venture. With JOBS Act, start-up companies can raise up to $1million in any 12 months period. Until now, social media sites cannot be used as a capital raising platform. Small businesses can now be able to solicit for business funds through the internet when the rules for implementation of JOBS Act are finalized by SEC.

Equity-based crowdfunding in Italy

Equity based crowdfunding received approval in Italy in July 2013 when the legislation was announced by the Italian Financial Authority. With the passing of the law, Italy became the first European country to implement crowdfunding laws. The purpose is to regulate activities of online platforms that facilitate raising of funds by instituting a framework that will reduce operational risk. The framework will in addition reduce legal risks to operators and other businesses.

Italy is implementing equity based crowdfunding with its own flavor by separating risk capital from debt capital. The implication is that equity based crowdfunding in Italy is for risk capital and not for debt capital. An important fact to note is that crowdfunding in Italy can only be permitted for what the decree described as "innovative startups". Equity based financing in Italy is biased in the favor of very high risk and high technology orientated companies.

Equity based crowdfunding platforms are required to apply for registration before they can be included in the register. A platform registered to operate in Italy for the purpose of equity crowdfunding is obliged to disclose certain information to investors, provide a questionnaire for investors to confirm their awareness of the high risk nature of the investment they are about to make. This is not taken as an investment advice because it is strictly forbidden for crowdfunding portals to give investment advice.

Rewards based crowdfunding platform

This type of crowdfunding platform requires less strict regulation than the equity. The business model for this is that the crowd who identifies with the project will not become a co-owner. The contributor can only get a stated reward. The reward may be tangible or intangible. A reward is typically a product or service. It is not measured in monetary worth of how much a contributor has pledged. It is left at the discretion of the campaigner to decide what constitutes a reasonable reward. It is important to note that contributors will only part with their money if they consider the reward to be reasonable.

Donation based crowdfunding platform

As the name implies the platforms that operate under this model are set up to assist organizations and individuals to raise funds from the crowd. Under a donation based crowdfunding model, an organization that wants to make a pitch may not have to give anything in return. The organization may on the other hand decide to give a gift as a way to show appreciation.

The platform will not insist that a project owner will specify a gift in return, it is left to the discretion of the project owner. Not for profit organizations and charities are the major users of this model of crowdfunding.

Debt based crowdfunding platform

Under this operating platform, the business model is for the platform to be set up as a loan facilitator. The platform brokers a loan between borrowers and lenders, which is the "the crowd". This business model is also referred to as peer to peer lending in some circles. The platform is set to accommodate both interest bearing and noninterest bearing loans. Debt based crowdfunding platforms allow the loan to be auctioned thereby giving the lenders an opportunity to determine and select the portion of the loan to lend. Lenders are able to choose either to lend to individual consumers or to business organizations.

Peer to peer lending platforms in the United Kingdom has been lobbying for the FCA to categorize and regulate their platforms like the way equity based platforms are regulated. This is because such regulation will help to increase the confidence that the crowd have on peer to peer lending platforms. The FCA is proposing for a framework for the regulation of peer to peer lending platforms in the future.

How crowdfunding platforms operate

Crowdfunding platforms have some operating principles in common in the way they operate irrespective of the business model they have adopted. Some platforms allow the project owner to keep all the sum of money contributed towards the project irrespective of whether the project meets its target or not. This is called the "Hold all" principle. While some platforms insist that only projects that meets its target can be able to keep the contributed or pledged funds. This is called "Threshold principle".

Threshold principle

When a project is launched, the project will be for a specified amount of money. That amount is the Target amount or Threshold. Backers can promise to pay a specified amount of money. If it is on a Threshold principle platform, the backers are only obliged to redeem the pledge if the Threshold or Target is reached within the agreed period.

Where the pledged funds have been redeemed before the end of the period, some platforms will transfer the pledged funds to an escrow account. Funds transferred to an escrow account are returned to the backers if the threshold is not met. If the project is met or exceeded, the funds in escrow account is then transferred to project accounts of campaigners.

Hold all principle

Crowdfunding platforms that operate the Hold all principle require the backers to redeem the pledge irrespective of whether the threshold was met or not. Some platforms do combine both the threshold principle and hold all principle in a way that meets their customer needs. Examples of sites that operate on the Hold all principle are Indiegogo, RocketHub and Sponduly.

Holding model

This involves the platform operator creating a subsidiary company as an individual holding for each of the crowdfunding ventures that are to be funded. Under this model, contributions from individual investors are pooled together as a single entity. Investments are made using the identity of that single entity. The objective is to enable a process that can protect the rights of individual investors that owns the investment.

The club model

The Club model is another creative way to circumvent the strict regulation of equity based crowdfunding platforms. Using this strategy, the crowdfunding platform will organize potential investors to form a club and have membership status of the club. Membership is usually strict by invitation and it operates in a closed circle like an investment club.

The framework for investment club allows the Club to bypass the strict regulatory framework for equity investment. This is because an investment club falls under the category of "informed investor". Qualified investors are regarded as sophisticated investors, thus they need less protection from the law. Though these sophisticated investors are members of the public who are supposed to need protection, the framework of investment club enables them to skip the tight ropes and complicated, time consuming regulatory procedures.

Equity crowdfunding checklist for investors

This is not an exhaustive list and it varies from country to country. However, the list below is some of the requirements that a company seeking for equity fund must meet before it is certified ready to campaign for equity fund.

Due diligence

Crowdfunding platforms are invested with the responsibility to protect the general public by performing some checks on any company that wants to pitch for funds through their platforms. The implication of this is that they could be held liable for any fraudulent project that is displayed to the public using their platform. Crowdfunding platforms are therefore required to have a robust business process that will enable them perform some background checks on a company, its' promoters, business objectives and many other checks that can be done to protect investors.

Ratings

As part of the due diligence service, crowdfunding platforms can use a rating system, whereby they rate each project. Then potential investors can use such ratings as a guide to determine their risk appetite.

Sample contract forms

Contractual agreements can be very tricky even when the project is a very good and genuine one. A badly drafted business agreement can make the difference between making a profit and making a loss. The cost of getting professionally drafted business contracts can be quite prohibitive, especially to micro investors. Crowdfunding platforms can go the extra mile to assist micro investors by drafting a prototype contractual agreement for different categories of projects on their platforms.

Protect investors

Platforms can help to protect investors by setting up a structure that can make it easier to protect the investor and the company they support. An example is how Seedrs crafted agreements that allow crowdfunding investors to have voting rights in companies. Seedrs also have a nominee structure that protects investor's right and facilitates effective management of investors for the companies that raised funds using Seedrs platform. Thus Seedrs plays a dual role to protect both parties and ensure that each party gets a good deal from the relationship.

Chapter 7

How to choose the right crowdfunding platform

The decision to embark on a crowdfunding campaign is not a decision to be taken lightly. There are certain characteristics that make one platform different from the other. Over the years, several crowdfunding platforms have emerged with the objective to serve diverse group of clients and to fill up gaps in areas that were not already represented in the crowdfunding market.

Chapter 4 has a good description of how crowdfunding works. It is packed with tips and necessary information about all you need to know before you embark on a crowdfunding campaign. As there are diverse groups of people requesting for funds from the crowd, to enable them fulfill their objective, so are there various models of crowdfunding. At this point in time, there are Equity, Debt, Reward and Donation based crowdfunding models. The models were discussed in detail in chapter 6. It is important to know about the models before you proceed with a campaign.

This chapter will give you a brief overview on how to highlight the summary of condition that is available under different crowdfunding models and the platforms. Due to the number of crowdfunding platforms that are already in business and even the many more that are yet to be established, this chapter will equip you to jumpstart your search for a suitable platform. The list is not exhaustive, but it is a good starting point.

A more robust list of crowdfunding platforms is available at www.crowdfundingsource.org robust list. The platforms listed in this chapter are not connected to the author in any way. Their listing in this book is not to be seen as a recommendation. It is rather an example of how to organize information about crowdfunding platforms for effective decision making

The table below is an example of how to collate information about platforms under different crowdfunding models. It also includes sample of the types of projects that they can take. Each platform has the number of days it allows a campaign to run. The commission structure is not the same across board. Some platforms charge commission on the project, while some platforms charge both the project and the investor. It is important to be armed with all these information to enable you make the right choice of model and platform.

Equity Based Platform

Platform	Project Type	Comm	Invest Period	Amount Variable
Crowdcube www.crowdcube.com	• Start up finance	5%	90 days	£5,000 or more
Startups www.crowdcube.com/ partner/startups/	• Start up finance	5%	90 days	
SeedUps www.seedups.com	• Technology • Start up finance	2% of successful investment plus 2% from investors profit	180 days	Under £500,000
Seedrs www.seedrs.com	• Pre-start finance	7.5% of successful investment plus 7.5% from investors profit	90 days	Under £150,000

Reward based platforms

Platform	Project Type	Commission	Investment Period	Amount Variable
Kickstarter www.kickstarter.com	• Startup projects	5%	70 days	No limit
	•			
Peoplefund. www.peoplefund.us	• Small scale & creative projects • Entrepreneurs • Ethical objectives	5%	90 days	No limit
Sponsume www.sponsume.com	• Creative ideas • Artists • Startup projects	4%	90 days	Minimum £200
Fundageek www.fundageek.org	• Pre-launch and early stage start ups • Research projects	5-9%	90 days	No limit
Buzzbnk www.buzzbnk.org	• Social enterprise related projects	Registration fee of £25 plus 5% of investment	90 – 180 days	Between £5,000 to £30,000
Indiegogo www.indiegogo.com	• Start ups • Creative projects • Philanthropic projects • Community projects • Health • Education	4% of successful investment or 9% of flexible funding campaigns	60 days for fixed funding and 120 days for flexible funding	No limit

To collate information about crowdfunding platforms in this way will provide an overview of what to expect. With this type of snapshot, it becomes easier to make informed decision.

Chapter 8

Crowdfunding intermediaries

Crowdfunding platforms are growing by the day, and so are the various types of unique service offerings available on them. Each crowdfunding platform has some unique offerings that differentiate it from the others. Even as the crowdfunding industry grows towards maturity, the service offerings and statutory regulations that guide those offerings are beginning to emerge. As the industry continues to grow, the bouquet of products and service offering will tailor the same growth pattern.

New group of experts are also emerging and they are currently creating strategies that will enable them to be positioned as the backbone of various crowdfunding communities. I have classified them into three categories.

Classification of intermediaries

The first group is supporting the crowdfunding industry by providing knowledge and expertise that they believe can aid successful crowdfunding campaign. Second categories of experts are providing support to ensure that what happens after a campaign can be managed in an ethically accepted fashion. The third category is crowdfunding industry experts that work within the legal framework of statutory regulations.

These groups of professionals are known by different titles and designations ranging from crowdfunding consultant, crowdfunding mentor, crowdfunding service provider and many others. There are still many unanswered questions about how these intermediaries will operate and how their services can be regulated.

Some other questions that are still awaiting answers are how to rate the performance of these intermediaries, and what will be the critical success factor. The first group of experts that offer knowledge and expertise on how to have a successful crowdfunding campaign emerged out of players in the ecommerce and social media. They provide support and advice ranging from how to choose the right technology and platform, how to plan a successful campaign, and how to reach out to potential donors and investors using the internet and social media.

Professionals that support crowdfunding industry with expertise on how to manage a business, manage funds and shareholders are emerging out of traditional financial industry players. Some of these are accountants and fund managers who created unique services for the crowdfunding industry. Those that are supporting the legal framework are emerging out of professionals from the legal profession. Some of these professional have been close to the financial industry and have been navigating the waters of compliance with statutory regulations over the years.

On a general note, these professionals claim to be able to help individuals and organizations to manage crowdfunding process. Whether these claims can be substantiated is still subject to further investigation, observation and discussion. This chapter is aimed at identifying those intermediaries, the services they claim to provide and how to protect your interest to enable you get a good service for your money.

Desperation to have a successful crowdfunding campaign is driving crowdfunding campaigners to seek the help and support of these intermediaries. Many of the campaigners are totally dependent on the support of crowdfunding intermediaries. The support ranges from writing of business plans, choice of technology platform, writing of marketing strategy and plan to preparation of financial documents and performance of due diligence.

Several more companies are developing different products and services to meet any conceivable need of crowdfunding industry. As is often the case with new industries, the players in the industry are re-segmenting their products or services to accommodate the needs of the industry while also creating a niche position for their business. While existing and potential new entrants into the crowdfunding arena are gearing up to connect with the growth of the industry, there are growing concerns about what will constitute performance on contractual agreements with crowdfunding intermediaries. This is because many state governments are still struggling with the issue of setting regulatory framework to guide various aspects of crowdfunding. Campaigners will have to devise how to protect their interest and that of their donors and investors.

How to engage crowdfunding intermediaries

Verify area of expertise

It is important to verify the industry that an intermediary has been servicing in the past. For example, an intermediary that has been providing marketing or promotion services in the technology industry is unlikely to take your campaign to the Promised Land, if it is targeted at the gaming industry. Consultants that are already experienced with the mechanics and requirements of your target industry are more likely to deliver a better return on your investment for hiring a consultant.

You can still hire a rookie and have a successful campaign. However, it is good to know who you want to engage their service. That will enable you manage your level of expectation. It can be very disappointing to find out after the campaign that your consultant did not have the expertise for your target market. Knowing the level of expertise for your consultant can also help to determine appropriate pay for the service.

Determine the best payment model

Consultants serving the crowdfunding industry have different ways of charging for their services. Some of the consultants charge hourly rate for the time they spend on a project. This is usually in addition to an initial consultancy fee. Another category of service providers charge fixed rate for the whole project time while some charges on commission basis. The ones that charge on commission basis will take a percentage of the amount raised on the campaign.

There is no best model. You may also consider a hybrid model where you can combine two or more models. It all depends on the type of project that is on campaign. The campaigner should have a way to determine the best model. All the models have their pros and cons. A few tips to note about payment options.

I.   Though fixed rate may look appealing because you can easily determine your upfront cost. It is very important to find out how many man hours the consultant can invest in the campaign. This is because the consultant may not have any motivation to work towards a successful campaign if the payment has been fixed upfront.

II. Commission based payment model gives the impression that consultants will be most motivated if they are to be paid a percentage of the campaign fund. While this is very appealing especially with the fact that there is no upfront fee, it is important to find out if the consultant has enough time and motivation to focus on the campaign. The consultant will still get paid the agreed percentage even if the consultant did not work for the pay.

III. Hourly paid payment options are better for use where there is a way to monitor the hours that the consultant logged for the project. This type of arrangement can be easy to get from consultants who render services through online job portals. Most freelance job portals have technology platform that enables logging of project hours. An access to a log of paid hours can enable a campaigner to verify logged hours. Online job portals like ODesk, Elance, Guru and Freelancer can be of great help.

Design a good job description

The need to hire a consultant is expected to stem from the fact that a thorough analysis of existing resources has been made. The analysis will reveal what is required, what is available and what will be required to meet the campaign objective. Job description in this concept will be written to show the type of resources required for the job.

Before you engage a consultant, write a good job description that will explicitly state the functions and activities of the consultant. If for example the consultant is expected to send 10 twitter broadcasts to 10,000 twitter users in a day, it should be clearly stated. It is not good enough to just write 'send twitter broadcast daily'. You need to state the target market for the tweet. A consultant with a followership of charity donors will not be described as having satisfied the requirement of the contract if the target market is equity investors. The implication is that a good job description for a consultant will include key performance indicators and how performance on the job will be measured.

Social status of the consultant

Crowdfunding relies heavily on the use of social networks. A would be marketing or public relations consultant must be a person or an organization that can boast of loads of numbers of followership on social networks. One of the keys to a successful crowdfunding campaign is ability to pre-plan and generate large numbers of followership on social networks.

The importance of social network status for a crowdfunding marketing consultant cannot be over emphasized because crowdfunding campaigns are driven through social networks. Information and news about crowdfunding campaigns are disseminated through various social networks. Crowdfunding thrives on connection with the crowd. A consultant with the right crowd can drive a campaign to meet its targeted objectives.

To ensure a good return on investment for hiring a consultant, you have to verify the claims for having large numbers of followers or being connected to the right crowd. There are possibilities that some consultants may claim to have more connections than they do. I recommend the use of site like statuspeople.com to verify authenticity of marketing and public relation consultants.

Chapter 9

Security of crowdfunding investment

Crowdfunding is driven by the explosion in the number of people that use social networks and in the increase in activities within social networks. Crowdfunding campaign projects are available for anyone that has access to the internet. The implication is that there are possibilities of fraud and theft of virtual and digital assets.

It is important that anyone that has considered crowdfunding as an option for investment must have special interest on how to protect digital and virtual assets. This chapter discusses some of the ways to ensure security of crowdfunding investments. Many state governments are still deliberating on what constitutes adequate protection, under protection and over protection of crowdfunding investors. While that discussion is ongoing, crowdfunding market is not halting to wait for the outcome of such deliberations. What that means is that individual investors will have to works hard at finding legal means to protect investment in crowdfunding.

Protect your intellectual property

If you are an investor, entrepreneur or enthusiast in any field of endeavor with an idea that you think can change the world, then that is your intellectual property. It is your brain child and you want to be able to manage and determine how that idea is used by anyone. Even if you are just a small business enterprise that is trying to raise funds to enable your business move to the next level, your time and money you have used to keep the business going is your investment. That investment will need some form of protection.

To protect that unique idea from being copied by others, you will need to find out from the patents authority in your locality or country if that idea can be protected. The Authority will also be able to give the necessary advice on how to protect your idea. Patent Authorities cannot assure you of protection for an idea that has been made publicly available. They are organizations that can protect ideas that have not been made available to the public. As soon as you publish the idea on a crowdfunding platform, it has become available to the public. You may not be able to protect it if you have not done that already.

If you are in doubt, seek legal advice from an intellectual property lawyer. The lawyer will be able to assist you to determine if your idea is patentable, and how to protect the idea with patent rights. Do not leave it to chance, you may lose the right to a world changing idea.

Use non-disclosure of agreement

A non-disclosure agreement is an agreement between two parties where one of the parties is the owner of a tangible or intangible idea or product and the other party has an interest to know about the product or idea. The party that is the owner writes some conditions indicating that the party that has an interest in the product or idea must not use the idea or disclose it to a third party without the consent of the owner. Unless you have the experience to draw up such legally binding document, it may help to seek the help and advice of a legal practitioner or any other business professional that has the experience to write a non-disclosure agreement with all the right clauses and conditions.

Some crowdfunding portals have been able to incorporate the use of non-disclosure of agreements into their business process. The importance of using a non-disclosure of agreement is to ensure that potential investors do not leave you out in the cold while they run with your idea. It is possible that a potential investor who has the money you need may tap into your idea, and develop it without your knowledge. If the idea becomes successful before you launch, you would have lost the market and profitability. You may even lose the right to promote the idea if it has been patented and protected by another person or business. At the point of trying to decide or make a choice of crowdfunding platform, do not forget to take that into consideration. Some platforms are able to make some areas of your campaign project to be password protected. The implication is that the password protected section of your campaign data is not available to the general public. That section can be only be accessed by people who met pre-determined conditions.

This is especially relevant to campaigners that cannot afford to hire the services of consultants that can write non-disclosure agreements. Crowdfunding portals may be able to provide that service without additional fee. Another way to use non-disclosure agreements is for hiring consultants. This is because a consultant or any other member of your team may likely have unrestricted access to all your business plan and strategy. It is important to ensure that whatever idea or plan that was shared with the consultant is protected.

You can protect your investment by ensuring that any business intermediary or associate is asked to sign a non-disclosure agreement. It is not 100% proof that your ideas are secured, bit it is a good measure of protecting an investment.

Protect your trademark

Your ideas are not the only assets that need protection. Any sign or logo that identifies your business or idea can become a good tool of differentiation between your business and other businesses. The need to get protection for your trademarks cannot be over emphasized. Investors in crowdfunding projects are to carefully examine trademarks of companies or projects they wish to support. If you invest on any business or idea that is based on a foundation of forgery or fraud, you may lose all your investment.

Due diligence

This is one activity that any serious investor must consider as a primary step to ensure protection of investment especially in crowdfunding investments. It is good practice for investors to perform some background checks on any business they want to support. It is important to check if the idea you want to support as an investor has been protected with patent rights. If you invest in a business that has not secured its intellectual property, you could end up losing your investments. If in doubt, ask the business to show proof that it has patent right over the idea it is promoting.

In the same way, campaigners must try to carry out background checks on crowdfunding platforms before making a decision to pitch a campaign on any crowdfunding platform. There have been some instances where campaign projects failed because the crowdfunding platform that was used did not have the capacity to publicize and create awareness for certain projects.

An example could be a crowdfunding platform that is under capitalized or has low publicity status on social networks. It will be difficult for such a platform to generate enough buzz and publicity that can create awareness for projects on its platform. With a little bit of digging deeper, you may be able to find out if the platform has the capacity to take up your type of project and make it a success. It does not matter how well you prepared for a project, or how beautiful your idea looks, it will not succeed without good publicity.

Many of the popular crowdfunding platforms has huge database of subscribers to their newsletter. The platforms send out regular broadcast about campaigns running on its platform. That is done to let people know that campaigns are running on a platform and also to solicit for support from the crowd. Other ways that crowdfunding platforms support campaigns are by running sponsored Ads on search engines like Google, Yahoo and several others. Sponsored Ads are also placed on social media sites like Twitter and FaceBook. The Ads are sent to specified target market. People in that category will see the advert irrespective of whether there is a social connection with the sender or not. A crowdfunding platform that lacks the financial capacity to engage in such promotions may not help your campaign.

Review the business plan

A business that wants to raise funds will in most cases have a business plan. It is your responsibility as an investor to review the plan. If you do not have the experience to review a business plan, get a professional help. Some of the basic facts that you may need to crosscheck are how they have utilized funds in the past and how the company intends to utilize the funds it wants to raise.

In some cases, the reason behind the motive could be different but you can detect it with a careful review of the plan. You may also use the information that you gathered from the business plan to ask for further clarification on other aspects of the business. A business plan is likely to have certain information like milestones it will achieve if the required fund is raised. To protect your investment, you can try to investigate if that milestone is achievable within stipulated time and budget. With such an investigation, you may be able to determine if the budget of time and resources are too low or too high.

Some companies may be aware that their budgets are not realistic. But because the company wants to make a very attractive offer, that will be easily acceptable by investors, it may use falsified information. You can save your investment from such fraud by investing time to review the business plan.

Develop an exit strategy

One of the best practices of sophisticated investors is that they have a clear plan on when to buy into an investment and when to exit from the investment. Small caps are traditionally known to be plagued with illiquidity. The shares can be a bit difficult to offload especially in the short run.

Most businesses that are raising equity capitals from crowdfunding platforms are small caps and will most likely have same issues associated with small caps. Decision to invest in a small cap should also be backed with the knowledge that exit may not be very easy in the short run. Before you invest in a company, decide how long you intend to hold the investment. Some companies have pre-determined exit strategy for investors. Ask if the company you want to buy their investment has such an option.

If they do have it, review the option and decide if it works for you. If not, feel free to negotiate for something that can suite your purpose. Even when the company decides not to discuss further on the issue, it is good to know your options before you invest in any company.

Chapter 10

Successful crowd campaign

The prospect of running a business or work on a project that will change the world can be very exciting. Even when you are already in business and need to move to the next level of your business, the thought of doing something new can still be exciting. In all situations, business finance and funding will be part of daily concerns. You will need to think through your business case to determine the type of finance that will meet your need.

Preparing to seek for fund can cause significant strain on your time and resources. You may need the services of some professionals to ensure adequate plan and preparation. Before you set off on a journey to start crowdfunding for your project, do some planning.

Determine the type of finance you need

If an entrepreneur or a startup business has a strong business plan that can get a favorable response from banks or other traditional finance brokers, it may be good to try that option before approaching crowdfunding platforms. In some cases, your business may need specialist type of finance like asset financing or invoice financing.

Such business cases may work better with finance brokers that are set up for working capital financing. Other options may be to apply for a government backed loan. This option usually has conditions and if your business did not meet up with stipulated conditions, you may not be eligible for such government backed funding.

Where you think that your project is eligible for government backed funding, you may do yourself a good favor by making your application at the earliest convenience. If however you are convinced that the alternative finance revolution called crowdfunding is your best option, then this chapter is for you. This chapter discusses how to plan, prepare and run a successful crowdfunding campaign.

Planning for a crowdfunding campaign

Though there are great opportunities for anyone with a unique idea to be able to raise funds from the crowd by listing a project on a crowdfunding platform, it is not an all comer's game. For a crowdfunding campaign to be successful, it requires good planning. This is because there has to be something about your campaign that should make it attractive and sticky. The attractiveness of your campaign will determine how many seconds or minutes that each member of the crowd may be willing to spend reading and discussing about the campaign. Attractiveness in this contest is not only about the beauty of the images or video. It is a comprehensive package that includes motive behind, the idea and the presentation of the idea.

Crowdfunding requires making a pitch to the crowd to solicit for funds. Consider the option of securing your intellectual property before you start the campaign. Chapter 9 has an in-depth discussion on how to secure your intellectual properties.

Write a business plan

A business plan could be written or unwritten, but there must a plan. If crowdfunding is your desired option for raising business finance, then your plan must be written. The crowd cannot connect with an unwritten plan. If you can write a good business plan without the need to hire a professional business advisory consultant, that will be great. There are many free templates that can help with the process of writing a business plan. It is always more advisable to hire professional service when you need to write a business plan. This is because professionals are already experienced in the art of writing business plans. In some cases, they have helped several other businesses like yours to achieve the same objective you are trying to achieve.

Features of a basic business plan

Executive summary
This is a very important part of a business plan. This part is best written as the last part but it

should be on the first page of your business plan. An executive summary gives a comprehensive overview of all that is in your business plan. It is best to limit it to about 2 pages. Most people may not have the time or the patience to read through your entire plan, but they will read the executive summary. If the executive summary has something worth investigating further, then they will go to the specific page and read further. Start with the objective and how much money you need to achieve stated objective. In clear terms state how much money you want to raise. This is because the amount of money you need for the project may be different from the amount you need.

Investors are profit oriented people, so state how much equity you are willing to release for potential investors. If you have an exit strategy designed for potential investors, this is the place to slot it into the executive summary. Discuss briefly about your target market and its potentials. This is the part the will help investors determine viability of your target market. Investors want to know if you have enough information about your target market. Another important aspect of an executive summary is the experience, knowledge and skill of the promoters of the business. Investors want to have the confidence that there are capable people that can manage the business to profitability. A brief history about the motives for engaging in the project can go a long way to help with creating a connection with the crowd.

Though it is not always required in a business plan but I believe it has a prominent place in crowdfunding. This is because some investors or contributors to a crowdfunding campaign are driven purely by emotional sentiments and not by economic reasons. Such investors may not have need for your operating statement before they will connect to your campaign. Be passionate in statement of your motives. In all cases present an optimistic view even when the numbers are saying the opposite. In conventional business circle, a lender will request to know about past experiences of the people behind a business. Be clear about your past experience, your ambitions and your future aspirations.

What problems or potential problems are you trying to solve? State the problems you identified in your target market including the solution you are proffering to resolve the problem. Sales and marketing plans are important to achieving your profit target. Give a brief overview of the sales target and how you intend to achieve the target through your marketing and operational plan. It helps to use a table to display snapshot of details of how the money will be used for the business.

Mission & Vision

A business plan ought to have a clear mission statement, core values and organizational or firm culture. Your mission will point to the direction through which you see the world.

Every business or individual have the core value that drives their activities. It is good practice to state the core values and ethics that uphold the business.

This aspect of the plan will help to weed out investors that have contrary views. It will also attract the right investors to your business. There are some ethical investors that will never invest in a business that has no written core values.

Economic environment

No business operates in a vacuum. There is need for thorough research on the operating environment of your business. Review the micro and macro-economic environment to enable you have a comprehensive grasp of what happens around your business, in your local community, around your country of operation and around the globe. It cannot be over emphasized that the world is now a global village. What happens in one part of the world can easily spread to other parts of the world.

Define your business in context of what is happening in your industry. Describe how your business idea fits into the industry and how it can add extra value to that industry or any other industry. If you can afford to buy research papers from industry experts, that will be a fantastic approach, but where not, you can still glean out enough information from the web.

Current position assessment and competitive environment

Your business is not likely to be the only business operating in your industry. Even where you are the first, there must other businesses doing something that can be used as a yardstick. Identify the businesses that are your competitors and find out what they are doing well. Use their performance to measure your business in terms of where you are and where you want to be.

The use of Strength Weakness Opportunities and Threat (SWOT) analysis to assess a competitive business environment is very critical to having a correct assessment of your business. It is important to make this assessment in great depth. It will help to highlight those grey areas of your idea and you can use the information to fine tune your idea.

It may not be possible to have a totally perfect idea or business process. But if you are able to identify your weakness and threats to the existence of your business, you can compete with your strength and opportunities and manage your weakness and threat.

Business strategic objectives and plan

A business plan should have information about how you intend to manage the business. Even where you cannot provide detailed information about your business focus and market penetration strategy, give a brief overview. Investors are interested in knowing how you intend to navigate the waters of business world. The ability to manage a business to success requires focus and plan. Business success cannot be achieved on an ad hoc basis. It needs consistency and continuous improvement.

Operational plan

The operational plan will show a potential investor how prepared you are to manage a business or project of a particular size. Small businesses are known to be plagued with issue of not having a robust business process. A good project could be marred by poor business process. The entrepreneur or the campaigner will need to work with a business advisory professional to design a good business process that can sustain effective and efficient management of the business.

The operational plan should include plans for required personnel for the business including those that will assist with the crowdfunding campaign. This aspect is very important because, some businesses had a successful crowdfunding project but they realized too late that they did not make provision for the campaign expenses. A mistake like that could hamper a smooth business take off.

Each identified human resource should have a detailed job description to highlight how that resource connects to the overall success of the business. This means that human resources required for the crowdfunding campaign should have been identified as a cost item in the startup cost analysis and in the projected operating statement.

Marketing plan

Marketing plans are equally a sore point facing many small businesses. Investors want to know how you intend to create awareness about your project. Businesses need sales for sustainability. A plan on how to generate sales is a core critical success factor. If possible, break the marketing and sales plan down to a week by week activity.

It is important to back all projections in the plan with a robust market research and reasoning. The services of a business broker may be required to value an existing business. Past performance of your business must be clearly and accurately presented. For startups that have no past record, the emphasis should be to highlight sales forecast and how it intends to achieve the sales forecast figure. In all cases, let the number of stakes holding you are willing to release be categorically stated.

Risk Analysis

There are inherent risks in all types of business. It will not make much sense to pretend that there are no risks to your type of business. In your business plan, identify the startup risk, operational risk, growth risk and financial risks. Discus with a business advisor to identify the risks and how to make provision to manage them as they arise.

It is better to be prepared than to be caught unawares. Sophisticated investors will decode the risks even if you do not own up about them. It will help your credibility to acknowledge what is obvious.

Financials

The financials are as important as the other aspects of the business plan. Some investors will find the financials more important that the other parts. It is good to have all the different parts. This will make it easier for all interested parties to identify the part that they want to use. Include startup expenses, operating statement, balance sheet, break even analysis and some business ratio analysis

Choose a platform

Chapter 6 discussed the different types of crowdfunding platforms and the type of business models available on crowdfunding platforms and chapter 7 discussed how to choose the right crowdfunding platform. Refer to the two chapters to enable you decide the type of platform you need for your campaign. Here are additional tips on certain facts you need to check before you choose a platform.

Due diligence

Every crowdfunding platform has its own unique type of investors. It is up to you to find out the type of investors that had been supporting projects on a platform of your choice. You will need to decide if those investors are the type of investors or supporters you are looking out for. Despite the fact that you need funds, remember that you cannot work with all types of investors.

Some investors and crowdfunding campaign supporters have character traits that you may not like to identify with. It is easy to check on profiles of supporters and investors. To carry out a check on profile of investors is not a cumbersome exercise. A little bit of investment in time can keep your business way from future embarrassment. Most crowdfunding platforms will have a section that is dedicated to basic guides on how it works. That is a good starting point in your due diligence on a platform. You are required to read the guides and the instructions.

A thorough understanding of how a platform works will save you a lot of trouble. Another good source of information about the process of using any crowdfunding platform can be found at the Frequently Asked Question (FAQ) section of the website. Website owners often use that section to clarify various aspects of their website or business.

Legal documentation

Crowdfunding business space is still growing, and it is expected to continue to grow at a faster rate than expected. Every growth has a down side. Several state governments are in the process of issuing legal statements on various aspects of crowdfunding especially as it relates to equity crowdfunding.

You are to check your state laws or regulations on crowdfunding. This is not limited to your area of abode but including the laws and regulations on the locality or country of domiciliation of the crowdfunding platform. That will help you to determine if your campaign is legal within the concept of the law of that locality. It is unlikely that genuine investors will have an interest in investing in an illegal project because that is a potential loss of investment and loss of credibility.

Pitch a crowdfunding campaign

As there are several hundred of crowdfunding platforms, so are there different specifications of how upload a campaign. Irrespective of the way a system is specified or designed to operate, there are basic facts that any crowdfunding campaign must showcase if it wants to be successful.

Project definition

A good title is the starting point to a successful crowdfunding outing. Give your campaign a very short and memorable title. A good title must be able to reflect the objective of your campaign. To make it easier for the crowd to have the interest to read your campaign pitch, give your project a short description in very few words. These are definitive words that should indicate the type of project and what it tends to achieve. It should also reflect whether the project is on-going or a one off project. This is a very important aspect of a crowdfunding campaign project. On-going projects are not allowed on many crowdfunding platforms.

The crowd will connect better with a project that has a defined boundary that an on-going nature. If you have a project that is on-going in nature, break it down to small chunks. It is best if projects have a boundary. Concentrate on one chunk of the project at a time. Crowdfunding is coming of age and the practices are being refined to reflect standard business practices.

Crowdfunding is no more at the stage where anyone can harness public fund without working to show a level of seriousness. In your project, define a very clear goal that can be Specific, Measurable, Articulate and Time based (SMART). It is difficult to go wrong with your project definition if it is SMART. With a clearly defined goal, it can be easy for investors and donors to relate with the goal. A project with an unclear goal will be decoded when sophisticated or seasoned investors carry out a due diligence on it. The funding goal must be well researched and explained in your business plan.

Time is of essence, do not try to set a campaign period to be too short or too long. Certain campaign will definitely require longer time frame. If for any reason, you have an interest on a platform that cannot allow a reasonable time for your campaign, it may be necessary to re-consider your option before your campaign goes live. It may be injurious to your campaign if you set a time limit that is too short.

Reward

Reward is a very important aspect of a crowdfunding campaign. Backers of a campaign are very much interested on what they can get for parting with their money. If it is a donation based campaign, the reward must be seen to be tangible by donors. In a debt-based campaign, the interest rate and the mode of payment of the interest must be commensurate with industry lending rate. Even when it is an equity based campaign, potential shareholders are looking out for something very special and unique from a company before they invest in the business. Other forms of rewards could be a sample of the product, tokens and personal recognition. In all situations, prepare to give out a reward that the recipients can consider to be worthy of their time and support.

Postage costs can be astronomical if not properly managed. It should be added to the total cost of the reward you want to give out to backers.

Multimedia creative

Rich multimedia creative is a very important aspect a crowdfunding campaign. Though it is not a compulsory requirement in crowdfunding portals, it is highly essential. The crowd seems to relate more with pictures and video especially in multimedia formats.

Multimedia creative in video format is one of the best you can have in a crowdfunding project. The format for the video can vary from one platform to another, but you can't go wrong with an MP4 format. Though creating a good video can be challenging, you can get a good video recording that will not break the bank by engaging services of freelancers. A good place to check is oDesk, Elance and Freelancer.com. There are many other good online job portals that have excellent freelancers.

Your video should be short and precise. A good story does not have to be long. In your video, just share your vision with an example to support the vision. Good background music is advisable as long as it did not drown your voice or the message you want to send out. If the music is not a FREE music, seek permission from copyright owner. Even when it is FREE, read the terms to ensure that it can be used for commercial purpose.

A must have requirement for a good video should be an introduction of who you are, why you are passionate about the project and what you intend to achieve. Remember that you are asking for support from the crowd, so state in clear terms what action you expect. If you need money as donation or contribution ask for money. Where you need investors to invest in your business let it be known that you are selling investment opportunities.

As stated earlier, reward is very important. Every human action has a motivation factor. In your video, tell the people what you have to offer in return. Then justify why the crowd should invest in your campaign. Finally, show your face in your video. The crowd wants to see you.

Create awareness for your campaign

A good project description and a beautiful video are very relevant to a successful campaign. However, a campaign cannot be successful if the crowd is not aware that your campaign is running on any crowdfunding platform. The level of awareness that you are able to create will to a great extent determine the success or failure of your campaign.

Creation of awareness for a crowdfunding campaign is not an event or activity you dabble into while the campaign is already underway. These are sets of activities you would have started long before you start your campaign. As soon as you are convinced that crowdfunding is an option you want to explore to raise that finance that will enable you move to the next level, start a plan on how to connect with the crowd in your target market.

Build network

A network in this instance is not necessarily members of your family or friends. They are very important but they are not the only ones you need for a successful crowdfunding campaign. The first sets of people you need to connect with are people in your target market.

Your target market would have been defined in your business plan.

If your business plan did not identify your market plan, this is the time to do that. You probably would need to revisit your business plan if your target market was not identified. In addition, you need to define a strategy to connect with that group. There are various ways to connect with your target market. Some of the options are to find out where they hang out, the social media they use, the issues and concerns they have and the topics they discuss. If you get all the above information, try to become an active participant in their discussion.

If you do not belong to any social network, the time to get involved and start generating a buzz is when you are about to start a crowdfunding campaign. If you wait until your campaign is already on before you connect with the crowd, you may be disappointed and frustrated at the result. Many successful crowdfunding campaigns are by individuals or organization that made the right investment in the crowd.

Start a discussion

When you are able to connect with likeminded people, it makes it easier to communicate with them. It will help to start talking to your network about your intended idea. This is a good a way to get a quality feedback.

Feedbacks from your network can help you to form good plans or even to fine tune the business plan. If you have hired an intermediary to assist with planning for your campaign, the feedback from your consultant will be an added advantage. It will be good if you can get your friends and family to assist with spreading words about your idea. Do not expose the entire idea unless you have received a patent right for it.

Announce the campaign

As a way to officially announce your intention to your network, write a nice and personal email message to let them know about your project. The best way to start is to get an email messaging software that can help to format a professional looking message. Your network includes family, friends, former school mates, professional colleagues, members of your social network, blogs and directories. A Twitter and FaceBook announcement will be very help. All the other social networks are very good places to announce your campaign.

This is where an email messaging software becomes helpful. If you have a personal Blog, use it to announce your forth coming campaign. A one – off email blast is recommended for all your contacts to announce the campaign date. Send a second email to announce when the campaign is live. Do not turn your announcement to spam. In your email, give receivers an option to unsubscribe. In that case only those that have an interest in your message will receive further messages from you.

A press release is a fantastic option that will help to spread the word faster. But if you cannot afford a paid press release, there are websites that offer free press release. Though crowdfunding is purely an internet based activity, do not hesitate to meet up with potential backers that you can reach offline.

Contact the press

Newspapers, TV and radio station are not to be left out in your preparation. It may seem like it will always cost like bomb to use the services of the traditional media houses, but I can assure you that it may not be that expensive. You may even be able to get a free announcement for your campaign. Contact the media houses in your locality or country and send them your campaign announcement.

Manage campaign

When the campaign starts, send an email blast to your contact list to confirm availability of the campaign. It is not out place to write a second press release to say that the campaign has actually started. If you can afford to do that, it will be an added advantage. Crowdfunding success requires wide publicity.

Broadcast on website

Design a landing page on your website where visitors can see the campaign message. Post campaign updates and information about the campaign on that page. The landing page should be bold and attractive. If you have used a crowdfunding platform that allows the campaign code to be embedded to an external website, embed it in a conspicuous section of the landing page.

Post on social networks

This is the time to get busy with the social networks. Send updates to all the networks that you are connected with. Ask people in your network to assist you with sending out messages to their contacts. It is better to concentrate on a few social networks where you can generate real buzz than to scatter your messages in several networks without making an impact.

Write blogs

If you have a blog, get busy with writing updates through the blog. Distribute your blog to blog directories. Generate an RSS from your blog and submit it to RSS directories. You may even get creative by sending your blog to webmasters of blogs in related categories. As you blast your campaign message, remember that spam is unethical and can easily drive away potential backers. Do not spam. It is better to try to build a newsletter list.

In your blog, embed a newsletter subscription form to enable people subscribe to receive further information about your business. If you have used good email marketing software, the updates of the campaign you post on your blog can be automatically mailed to your subscribers.

Constant updates

It is very important to send constant updates through all the media you are using to raise awareness for your campaign. This could open a line of discussion with your network or other interested parties. Acknowledge those that backed your campaign even when the campaign is still on going. People feel good when there is a show of appreciation.

In some cases some backers can contribute twice or more to help a campaign succeed. Post the acknowledgement on your social network page, and also send them personal thank you note if you have their email address. It is important to maintain the relationship you have created or those you are about to cultivate. Some contacts may desire to communicate via emails, so do not forget to check your mails on a regular basis. A delayed email response may make the difference between a successful and a failed campaign.

Keep the momentum and keep your backers and your supporters informed. You may share comments and conversations that will not infringe on any one's privacy.

Manage campaign result

Irrespective of the outcome of your campaign, there are a few closing activities that you have to complete. Just bear in mind that a failure in one campaign is not an indication of failure of your business or your idea. Crowdfunding is not a one off activity. You can stage a crowdfunding campaign as many times as you want.

Appreciate your supporters

A campaign project requires the help of several people. As you wrap up the process, send a note to all that supported in one way or the other, to say thank you. This is very important because you may likely need their support in another way. Even when the campaigned did not meet its target, it is still good to keep your supporters happy by letting them know that you appreciate their efforts at helping you to meet your target.

Celebrate success

Success must be celebrated in a nice way. If you meet or exceed your target, share the good news. Blast the message on a press release, email, social network and any other medium you can think of. People want to be part of a success story. It is good to get the crowd involved, by asking them to contribute their opinion on how they want you to celebrate. That will help to create a sense of belonging and recognition.

Promise fulfillment

As you celebrate, do not forget the promise of a reward. This is a very crucial part. If the reward items are not readily available, send mails to all and keep them informed about what you are doing to get the reward ready. It could be overwhelming to arrange all the postings, but if you stay focused and organized, you will surmount the task.

There has been very poor management of reward fulfillment by people that met their campaign targets. I am led to believe that it was due to lack of prior planning. Some were due to poor planning because they did not take postage cost into consideration. If you have a good business plan, all the relevant cost would have been articulated and added up.

The End

Appreciation

You have reached the end of this book. Thank you for reading. If you found this guide useful, please share it with others. I welcome your suggestions and feedbacks.

Kindly connect with me.

@successpros

Thank you